W9-CGW-761

NA1

NATURE'S DESIGN
A PHOTOGRAPHIC ESSAY

by
Theodore D. Walker
A.S.L.A.

PDA Publishers Corporation

Additional copies may be ordered from: **PDA PUBLISHERS CORP.**
Box 3075
West Lafayette, Indiana
47906

Printed in the United States of America

To begin...

 The collection of photographs which forms this essay was gathered by the author over a period of years while traveling throughout the United States. The distance of the camera to the object varies from a few inches to a few feet thus representing a relative closeup view. Included are such objects as sand and rock; the trunks, bark, branches, and foliage of plants; ice, snow, and frost; moss and fungi; and clouds, sky, and water.

4

5

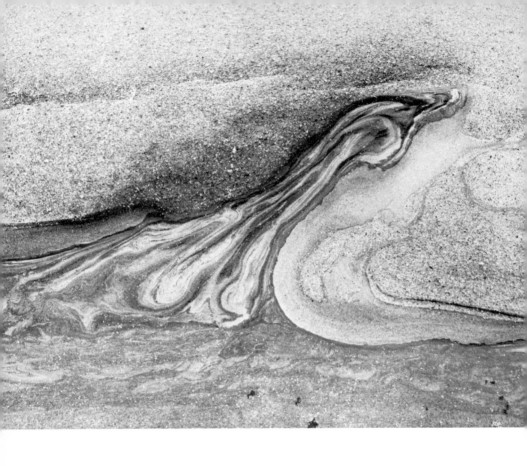

6

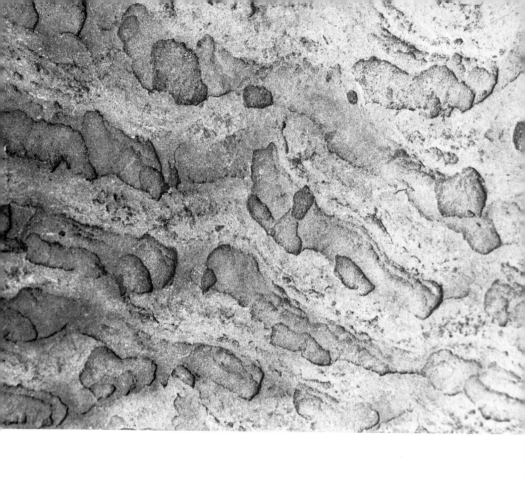

7

8

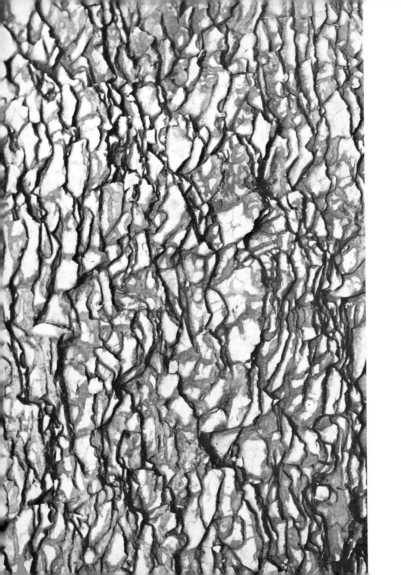

10

11

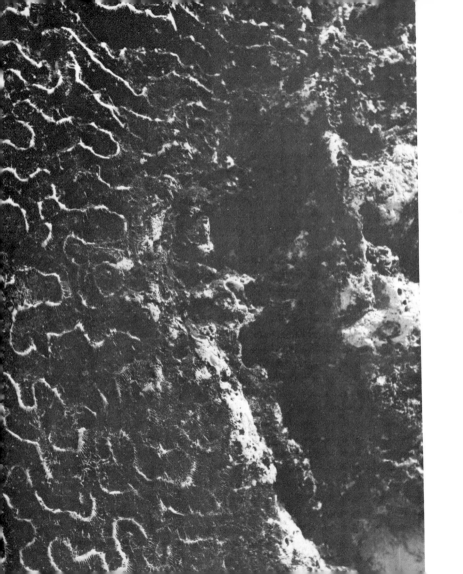

12

13

14

15

16

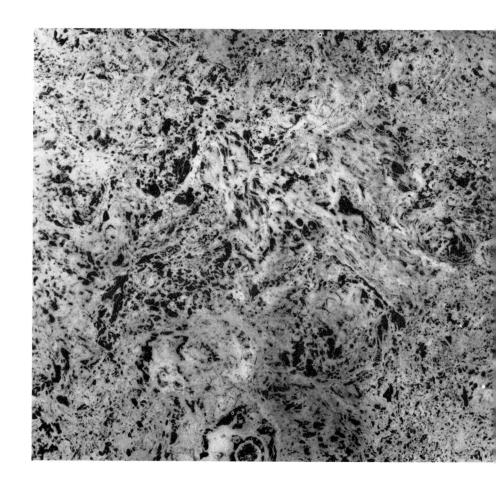

18

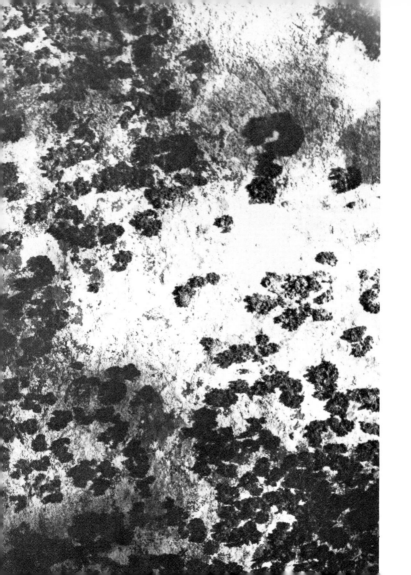

20

22

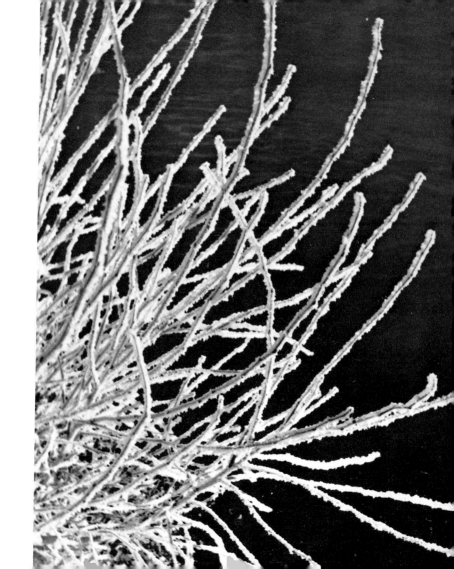

23

24

26

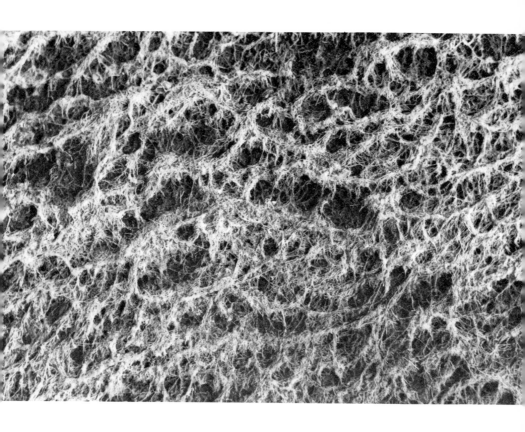

27

28

29

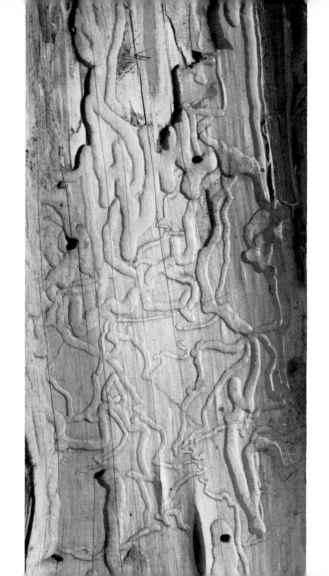

30

31

32

33

34

35

36

37

38

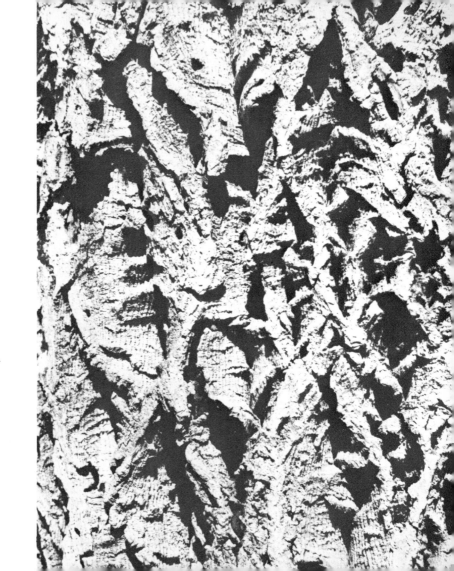

39

40

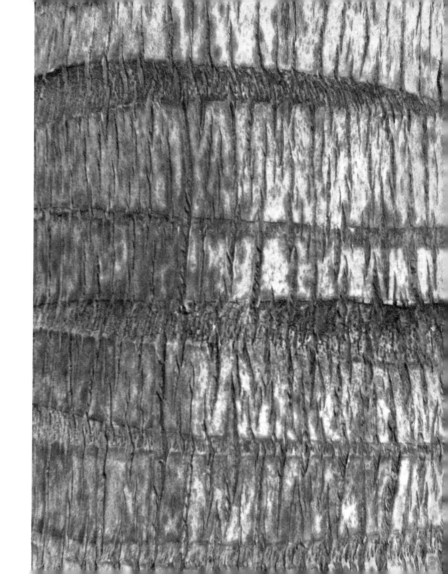

41

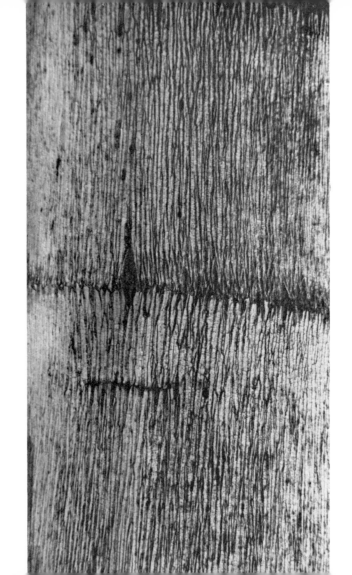

42

43

44

45

47

48

49

50

51

52

54

56

60

62

64

65

66

67

68

71

72

73

74

79

80

82

83

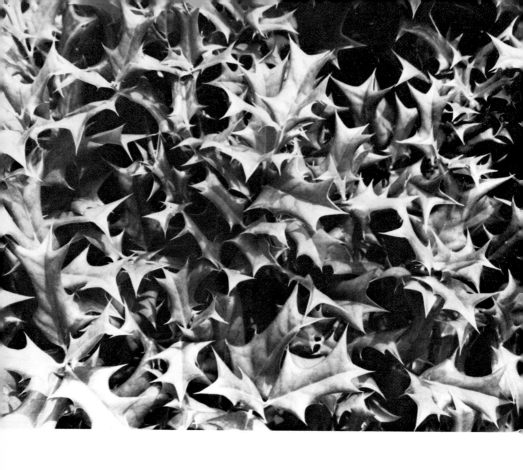

84

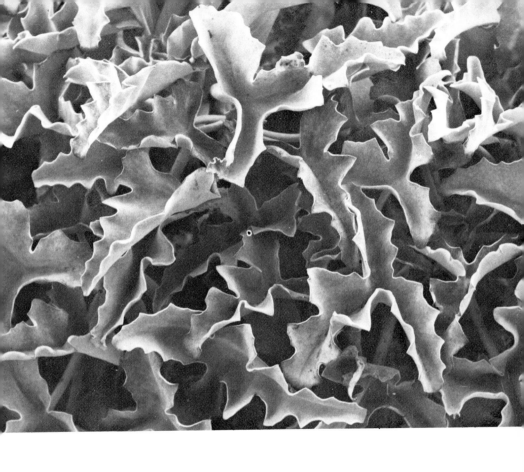

85

89

90

94

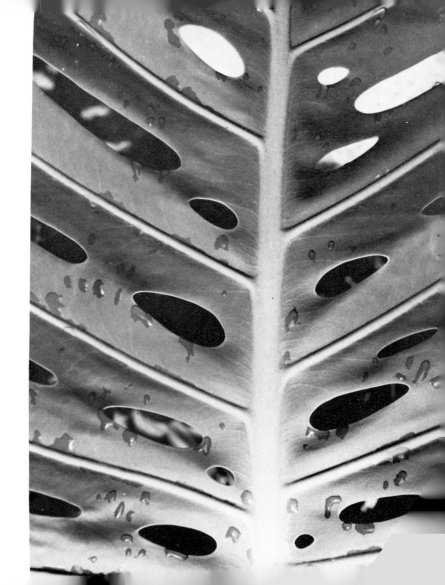

95

103